# Little Stars
# ICE SKATING

## A CRABTREE SEEDLINGS BOOK

Taylor Farley

**CRABTREE**
PUBLISHING COMPANY
WWW.CRABTREEBOOKS.COM

I can ice skate!

I skate at the **rink**.

My ice skates have
metal **blades**.

**blade**

The blades make it easier to move on the ice.

8

I hold my arms out to help me **balance**.

I push forward with one foot, then the other foot.

I like to do **dips**.

I like to do **spirals**.

17

I wore a helmet when I was a beginner.

One day, I would like to **compete**.

# Glossary

**balance** (BAL-uhnss): When you balance, you stay in a steady position and don't fall.

**blades** (BLAYDZ): Blades are the metal parts attached to the bottom of ice skates.

**compete** (kuhm-PEET): To compete is to try hard to win in a contest against others.

**dips** (DIPS): A dip is moving on the ice, with your feet about hips width apart, bending your knees as deeply as you can.

**rink** (RINGK): A rink is a large smooth area for skating. Ice rinks are covered in smooth ice.

**spirals** (SPY-ruhlz): A spiral is gliding on one foot, while raising the other foot above hip level.

# Index

# School-to-Home Support for Caregivers and Teachers

Crabtree Seedlings books help children grow by letting them practice reading. Here are a few guiding questions to help the reader build his or her comprehension skills. Possible answers are included.

## Before Reading

- **What do I think this book is about?** I think this book is about ice skating. It might tell us about different ice skating moves, like the one on the cover.

- **What do I want to learn about this topic?** I want to learn about how children learn to ice skate.

## During Reading

- **I wonder why...** I wonder why blades make it easier to move on the ice.

- **What have I learned so far?** I I learned that ice skaters hold out their arms to balance. They push forward with each foot.

## After Reading

- **What details did I learn about this topic?** I learned about two ice skating moves called dips and spirals.

- **Write down unfamiliar words and ask questions to help understand their meaning.** I see the word *rink* on page 5 and the word *compete* on page 21. The other vocabulary words are listed on pages 22 and 23.

Library and Archives Canada Cataloguing in Publication

Title: Little stars ice skating / Taylor Farley.
Other titles: Ice skating
Names: Farley, Taylor, author.
Description: Series statement: Little stars | "A Crabtree seedlings book". | Includes index. |
  Previously published in electronic format by Blue Door Education in 2020.
Identifiers: Canadiana 20200378929 | ISBN 9781427129819 (hardcover) | ISBN 9781427129994 (softcover)
Subjects: LCSH: Skating—Juvenile literature.
Classification: LCC GV850.223 .F37 2021 | DDC j796.91—dc23

Library of Congress Cataloging-in-Publication Data

Names: Farley, Taylor, author.
Title: Little stars ice skating / Taylor Farley.
Other titles: Ice skating
Description: New York, NY : Crabtree Publishing Company, [2021] | Series:
  Little stars: a Crabtree seedlings book | Includes index.
Identifiers: LCCN 2020049304 | ISBN 9781427129819 (hardcover) | ISBN 9781427129994 (paperback)
Subjects: LCSH: Skating--Juvenile literature. | Ice skating--Juvenile literature.
Classification: LCC GV849 .F25 2021 | DDC 796.91--dc23
LC record available at https://lccn.loc.gov/2020049304

## Crabtree Publishing Company

www.crabtreebooks.com          1–800–387–7650

Written by Taylor Farley

Production coordinator and Prepress technician: Samara Parent

Print coordinator: Katherine Berti

e-book ISBN 978-1-947632-43-1

Print book version produced jointly with Blue Door Education in 2021          Printed in the U.S.A./012021/CG20201102

Photo credits: Cover© Sergey Nivens;  pages 2-3 © katacarix; pages 4-5 © Radu Bercan; pages 6-7 and 16-17 © Arina P Habich; page 8-9 © Pavel Ilyukhin; pages 10-11 © Tomsickova Tatyana; Pages 14-15 © Vladimir57; Pages 18-19 © FamVeld; Pages 20-21 © Sergey Nivens
All photos from Shutterstock.com

**Published in Canada**
**Crabtree Publishing**
616 Welland Ave.
St. Catharines, Ontario
L2M 5V6

**Published in the United States**
**Crabtree Publishing**
347 Fifth Ave.
Suite 1402-145
New York, NY 10016

**Published in the United Kingdom**
**Crabtree Publishing**
Maritime House
Basin Road North, Hove
BN41 1WR

**Published in Australia**
**Crabtree Publishing**
Unit 3 – 5 Currumbin Court
Capalaba
QLD 4157

24